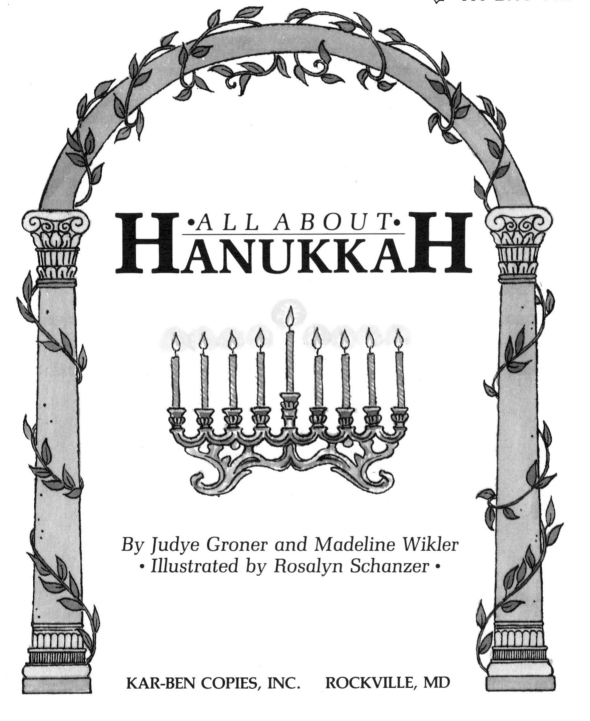

·ALL ABOUT· HANUKKAH

By Judye Groner and Madeline Wikler
· Illustrated by Rosalyn Schanzer ·

KAR-BEN COPIES, INC.   ROCKVILLE, MD

LIBRARY OF CONGRESS
Library of Congress Cataloging-in-Publication Data

Groner, Judyth Saypol.
   All about Hanukkah / by Judye Groner and Madeline Wikler; illustrated by
Rosalyn Schanzer.
      p.   cm.
   Summary: Discusses the historical background for Hanukkah and examines its
blessings, music, games, and modern observance.
      ISBN 0-930494-81-4: $10.95.   ISBN 0-930494-82-2 (pbk.): $4.95
   1. Hanukkah—Juvenile literature. [1. Hanukkah.] I. Wikler, Madeline,
1943-   . II. Schanzer, Rosalyn, ill. III. Title.
BM695.H3G68 1988
296.4'35—dc19   88-13435

CONTENTS

THE STORY OF HANUKKAH

Hanukkah was first celebrated over 2,000 years ago. The Jewish people were living in the land of Israel, which in those days was called Judea. Its capital and most holy city was Jerusalem. For many years, the Jews worked hard to build a beautiful Temple there. On Shabbat and the festivals, they came to the Temple to pray. They brought baskets filled with fruit and other gifts, and put them on the Temple altar.

The Jews of Judea were not free. They were ruled by the kings of nearby Syria. For a time, these rulers let the Jews pray to God, celebrate the Jewish holidays, and follow the laws of the Torah.

Then a cruel king, Antiochus, came to power. He followed the Greek religion, and wanted everyone to believe as he did.

The Greeks of long ago worshipped many gods. They believed there was a god who made the sun shine, another who made the flowers grow, and still others who made it rain and thunder. They believed they knew what their gods looked like, and built statues, called idols, in their homes and temples.

The Jews believed then, as they do now, in one God. They believe that you cannot see God, and that you cannot build statues or draw pictures of what you think God looks like. The Jews refused to follow the Greek religion.

Antiochus expected everyone to obey him. He
sent messengers to all the cities of Judea, ordering
the Jews to change their names to Greek names,
wear Greek clothes, and eat Greek foods. He

ordered them to put Greek idols in front of their homes and pray to them. Some Jews obeyed the king's orders because they were afraid to be different. But many refused.

Antiochus was very angry at the Jews who would not change. He ordered his soldiers to march into Jerusalem. They destroyed homes and set fires in the streets. They stormed the Temple and tore down the Holy Ark. They built a Greek idol and put it on the Temple altar.

Many Jews were killed. Others took shelter in nearby villages.

The soldiers went from town to town making sure the king's orders were being followed.

One day, they came to Modi'in, a town not far from Jerusalem. They built an idol in the marketplace and called the Jews together to pray to it. The town leader, Mattathias, refused to bow down to the idol. He raised his sword and turned to the people of Modi'in. He told them he would continue to believe in one God and obey the laws of the Torah. He called on the Jews to follow him.

Mattathias, his five sons, and many of the Jews fought off the soldiers and escaped to the nearby mountains. They knew that to be free they would have to defeat the king and his army.

But Mattathias was old and sick. Before he died, he gathered his sons—Yohanan, Simon, Judah, Eleazar, and Jonathan—and blessed them. *"Hazak ve'amatz,"* he said to them in Hebrew. "Be strong and brave."

Mattathias appointed his son Judah to be the new leader. Judah was called *Maccabee*, which means "hammer," and his followers became known as the Maccabees.

It was hard for Judah to form an army. The Jews were farmers, shepherds, and teachers. They were not trained to be soldiers. They had no uniforms and few weapons.

But the Maccabees knew the hills, caves, and countryside of Judea. They could move quickly and were able to surprise the king's army, even at

night. Most important, they were fighting for something they believed in. Their love for freedom gave them courage, and they fought long and hard.

The Maccabees went from village to village, defeating the Syrians and taking their weapons and uniforms. King Antiochus sent more and more soldiers, but the Jews drove them away.

Finally, the Maccabees reached Jerusalem. They went first to the Holy Temple. Its walls were crumbling. Weeds were growing in the courtyards. A Greek idol stood on the altar.

The Jewish fighters became builders. They scrubbed and polished the stone walls, cleaned the courtyards, and planted new trees. They took away the idols and built a new altar. They found iron spikes and put small torches on them to make a new menorah. At last, they were ready to celebrate.

On the 25th day of the Hebrew month of Kislev, exactly three years after the Syrian soldiers destroyed Jerusalem, the Jews lit the menorah and rededicated the Temple. For eight days they celebrated joyfully. The Maccabees proclaimed that every year the Jews should celebrate a holiday of rededication, now called Hanukkah.

Hanukkah is a celebration of miracles. Wonderful things happened which the Jewish people didn't expect. Even though the Maccabees were a very small army with few weapons and no experience, they were able to win over the very large, well-trained Syrian army. This was a miracle.

According to legend, when the Jews searched for the special, pure oil needed to light the menorah, they were able to find only one jug, enough to burn for just one day. But the oil lasted and lasted, and the menorah burned brightly for eight days. This, too, was a miracle.

HANUKKAH TODAY

All over the world, Jewish families gather each year to celebrate Hanukkah. For eight nights, they light and bless the festive candles to recall the ancient miracles. They exchange gifts, play dreidel, eat latkes (potato pancakes), and retell the story of the victory of the Maccabees and the little jug of oil that burned for eight days.

In Israel, a menorah shines from every office building, school, synagogue, and Jewish home, growing brighter each night as another light is added. At Modi'in, the ancient home of the Maccabees, torches are lit and carried by runners to cities throughout the land. Torches from Modi'in are also flown to other countries where they are relit and carried to synagogues and Jewish centers for Hanukkah celebrations.

CANDLE-LIGHTING

The Hanukkah menorah—called a *hanukkiyah*—should be lit at sunset and placed near a window, so that people passing by can see the lights. Hanukkah candles may not be used for anything but enjoyment, so a *shamash*, a helper candle, is used to light the others.

On the first night, light the shamash plus one, on the second night, the shamash plus two, and so on. You will need 44 candles for all eight nights. Candles should be lined up from right to left. But the last candle added is the first lit, and the lighting continues from left to right.

On Friday night, light the Hanukkah candles before the Shabbat candles. You should not do any work (not even homework!) while the lights are burning. Just relax and have fun!

In some families, everyone lights his or her own hanukkiyah. In other families, children and parents take turns lighting the candles.

CANDLE BLESSINGS

We say two blessings each night when we light the hanuk-kiyah:

בָּרוּךְ אַתָּה יְיָ אֱלֹהֵינוּ מֶלֶךְ הָעוֹלָם אֲשֶׁר קִדְּשָׁנוּ
בְּמִצְוֹתָיו וְצִוָּנוּ לְהַדְלִיק נֵר שֶׁל חֲנֻכָּה.

Baruch Atah Adonai Eloheinu melech ha'olam asher kideshanu bemitz-votav vetzivanu lehadlik ner shel Hanukkah.
We praise You, Adonai our God, Ruler of the Universe, Who makes us holy by Your mitzvot and commands us to light the Hanukkah candles.

בָּרוּךְ אַתָּה יְיָ אֱלֹהֵינוּ מֶלֶךְ הָעוֹלָם שֶׁעָשָׂה נִסִּים
לַאֲבוֹתֵינוּ בַּיָּמִים הָהֵם בַּזְּמַן הַזֶּה.

Baruch Atah Adonai Eloheinu melech ha'olam she'asah nisim la'avoteinu bayamim hahem, bazeman hazeh.
We praise You, Adonai our God, Ruler of the Universe, for the miracles which You performed for our ancestors in those days.

On the first night, we add this blessing:

בָּרוּךְ אַתָּה יְיָ אֱלֹהֵינוּ מֶלֶךְ הָעוֹלָם שֶׁהֶחֱיָנוּ וְקִיְּמָנוּ
וְהִגִּיעָנוּ לַזְּמַן הַזֶּה.

Baruch Atah Adonai Eloheinu melech ha'olam shehecheyanu, vekiyemanu, vehigiyanu lazeman hazeh.
We praise You, Adonai our God, Ruler of the Universe, Who has kept us alive and well so that we can celebrate this special time.

FREE TO BE

The Maccabees rose up against King Antiochus because he would not let them live as Jews. Throughout history, Jews have been forced to escape countries where they were not allowed to practice their religion. Perhaps your grandparents, aunts or uncles, were among them.

Even today, some Jews are not free. There are Jews in Arab lands, Ethiopia, and the Soviet Union who cannot celebrate Jewish holidays, pray in synagogues, or go to Jewish schools. These Jews have shown great courage. Many celebrate holidays and study Hebrew in secret. They continue to ask their government to let them move to a country where they can live openly as Jews.

Some people light an extra menorah each night of Hanukkah to remember these families.

FREE TO BE DIFFERENT

King Antiochus ordered the Jews in his kingdom to believe in the Greek religion. Many obeyed because they were afraid to be different. But the Maccabees believed it was wrong to give up their religion and copy another people.

Being Jewish today means being different. We celebrate Shabbat and Jewish holidays at home and in the synagogue. Our non-Jewish friends celebrate different holidays.

Around the same time Jews celebrate Hanukkah, our Christian neighbors are celebrating Christmas, a very holy day in their religious year. Because there are many Christians, we notice Christmas a lot—in homes, shopping centers, on television, and even in school. Even though no one is ordering us to give up our religion, at Christmas time especially, it can be hard for a Jewish person to be different.

- How do you feel about being Jewish at Christmas time?
- Do you ever wish you weren't different?
- Have you ever talked with your classmates or friends about Hanukkah and other Jewish holidays? Do you feel proud to be a part of Jewish history?
- How do you think Judah Maccabee would have felt about being different if he were living as a Jew today?

DREIDEL

The most popular Hanukkah game is dreidel. The dreidel is a spinning top. Its name in Yiddish means "turn." The Hebrew word for dreidel is *sevivon*.

There are four letters on the dreidel:  ש ה ג נ

They stand for the words, *Nes Gadol Hayah Sham*, which means "A Great Miracle Happened There."

Dreidels in Israel have these letters: פ ה ג נ

They stand for the words, *Nes Gadol Hayah Poh*, which means "A Great Miracle Happened Here."

Rules for playing dreidel:

Everyone starts with an equal number of nuts, raisins, or Hanukkah gelt. Each player puts one of these in the middle. The first player spins the dreidel. If it lands on:
    נ Nun—the player does nothing
    ג Gimmel—the player takes everything in the middle
    ה Hey—the player takes half
    ש Shin—the player puts one in

An easy way to remember is:
    נ N = nothing
    ג G = get
    ה H = half
    ש SH = share

Before the next player spins, everyone puts in another piece.

DREIDEL VARIATIONS

- See who can keep a dreidel spinning the longest. Time the spins with a stop watch.

- Try spinning the dreidel upside down.

- Let everyone spin a dreidel. Those whose dreidels land on the same letter get a point. Play to a specified number of points.

- Hebrew letters stand for numbers: Nun is 50; Gimmel is 3; Hey is 5; and Shin is 300. (On an Israeli dreidel, Pey is 80.) Take turns spinning the dreidel, and after each spin, record each player's score. See who can get to 1,000 first.

- Dreidel hunt: One player leaves the room while the others hide a dreidel. The player returns to hunt for the hidden dreidel, while the rest sing a Hanukkah song. As the searcher comes closer to the hidden dreidel, the singing grows louder; as he or she moves away, the singing gets softer.

GIFTS, GELT, AND GIVING

When your grandparents were children, they probably received coins—Hanukkah gelt—from their parents, aunts, and uncles. Today, many families exchange gifts as well.

While it is fun to receive gifts, it is thoughtful to give them to those we love. Homemade cookies, pictures, and crafts are special, because the person will know you took time to make them yourself. Another welcome gift is a promise to do something helpful—babysit, make your bed, or set the table.

Hanukkah is also a time for *tzedakah*—helping those in need. Set aside some of your Hanukkah gelt or allowance to put in the tzedakah box at home or school. Suggest that your class plan a Hanukkah party at a nearby nursing home or hospital.

When you receive your Hanukkah presents, remember to say thank you. Write a note or draw a picture and sign your name.

HANUKKAH RECIPES

On Hanukkah it is customary to eat latkes *(levivot)* and doughnuts *(sufganiyot)*. These foods are fried in oil and remind us of the miracle of the jug of oil that burned for eight days.

POTATO LATKES

Ingredients:

2 c. grated potatoes
Small onion
2 eggs

2 Tbsp. flour or matzah meal
1 teaspoon salt
Oil for frying

Grate potatoes and place in bowl. Grate in onion. Add eggs, matzah meal, and salt. Drain off excess liquid. Drop by spoonfuls into well-oiled frying pan. Fry on both sides in hot oil. Serve with applesauce or sour cream.

SUFGANIYOT (DOUGHNUTS)

Ingredients:

¾ c. orange juice or water
¼ lb. margarine
4 Tbsp. sugar
2 pkg. dry yeast

3 c. flour
2 eggs, beaten
Dash of salt
Powdered sugar and cinnamon

Combine orange juice, margarine, and sugar and heat until margarine melts. Cool to lukewarm and add yeast. Stir until dissolved. Combine all ingredients and mix. Knead until smooth. (You may need to add more flour.) Place dough in greased bowl and cover. Let rise in a warm spot for 30 minutes. Punch down. Shape small pieces of dough into balls, rings, or braids. Cover and let rise another half hour. Deep fry in hot oil. Drain. Put a few teaspoons of powdered sugar and cinnamon in a paper bag. Add doughnuts and shake.

REMINDER: *Cooking with hot oil can be very dangerous. Make sure that a grown-up is helping you.*

BLESSINGS

TRADITIONAL

1. Ba - ruch a - tah A - do - nai E - lo - he - nu me - lech ha - o -
2. Ba - ruch a - tah A - do - nai E - lo - he - nu me - lech ha - o -

lam, A - sher kide -sha - nu be — mitz - vo - tav vi - tzi -
lam, She - a - sah ni - sim la - a - vo - te - nu ba - ya -

va - nu le - had - lik ner shel_____ Ha - nu - kkah.
mim _____ ha - hem ba - - - zeman ha - zeh.

Ba - ruch a - tah A -- do - nai E - lo - he - nu me - lech ha - o - lam she -

he - che - ya - nu ve - ki - ye - ma - nu ve - hi - gi - a - nu la - zeman ha - zeh.